• TEACHERS •

•TEACHERS•

Life At The Chalkface

Special Edition for PAST TIMES® Oxford, England

Robinson Publishing Ltd.
7, Kensington Church Court
London W8 4SP

This edition published by arrangement with Punch Ltd.
copyright © Punch Limited 1998

*A CIP catalogue record of this book is available
from the British Library*

ISBN 1–84119–007–1

Design and computer page make up
Penny Mills
Printed and bound in the EC

CONTENTS

'Back to the old brain-washing again,
I suppose.'

THE
• NEW TERM •

HINTS TO SCHOOLMASTERS
[1845]

Towards Christmas and Midsummer it is necessary to advertise or send round circulars, or your school will never be able to stand the competition of of those semi-public establishments which are now so numerous. A good pretext for an advertisement is the re-commencement of school after the vacation; and though you may have only half-a-dozen boys, you may as well apprise them of the period for assembling, through the medium of the *Times* newspaper. You should always say you expect 'your young friends to re-assemble;' for though you may have been whacking your 'young friends' all through the last half-year, and have laid in two or three avenging birch brooms with a view to the next, there is something peculiarly attractive to parents in the mode of address alluded to. If you want pupils, say the number is limited – which it very likely will be – and never let there be a vacancy for more than two, for it is not likely that more than two will be sent from the same family, and each parent should be made to feel a sort of privilege in having room found for his child or children.

Small boy (about to return to school): 'Well, goodbye Mummy dear.'
Mother: 'But darling, of course I'm coming to the station.'
Small boy: 'I know, Mummy, but I thought if we got the worst over here we might part decently at the station.'

Always make the nominal terms as low as possible, for it is easy to stick it on in extras, as the following sample of a school-bill will testify:

J Spooner, Esq. Dr.   To J. Whackum:

	£		
To half a year's board and tuition	£9	9	0
Geography, with the use of the Globes	1	1	0
Simple Mathematics, with the use of			
the Compasses	1	1	0
Belles Lettres and broken windows	1	1	0
Classical rhetoric and washing	2	2	0
Algebra and the use of the skittles	1	1	0
Dancing and drilling	1	1	0
Extra for the Polka	0	10	6
German master and dentist	1	1	0
Dancing master and medical attendance	1	0	0
Extras during the half year	2	2	0
Share of breakage	0	10	6
	22	0	0

This arrangement enables you to advertise your terms as eighteen guineas per annum, while you in fact make them upwards of four-and-forty.

As it is desirable to be able to announce that there are certain exhibitions attached to the school, it would not be a bad idea to make an arrangement with Madame Tussaud, the Chinese Collection, and one or two more for a season-ticket for half-a-dozen, so that the boys might be taken in turn; and though these are not the sort of

'This proves what I've always maintained: Parents are precisely the people who ought not to have children.'

exhibitions that the parents would desire, the pupils would no doubt be perfectly satisfied.

Get a Master of Arts, if you can, to enable you to advertise his name as an assistant, with M.A. at the end of it. Masters of Arts may be had very cheap now, from the Scotch or Irish Universities, and they give great respectability to an establishment.

If you send out holiday letters, let them be written in one or two different languages; and the following would give the parents an idea of juvenile classical proficiency:

Μι δεαρ Παρεντς,

Ουρ ὀλιδαις κομμενσε νεξτ ωεεκ, ανδ ι ὀπε το φινδ ιου ανδ αλλ θε φαμιλι χυιτε ωελλ.

ιουρ αφφεκτιονατε σον

Αρθυρ Βροων

Of course a letter of this description must only be sent to a parent who is not likely to detect the humbug of it; and if it is pointed out to him, you must declare it was intended merely to exercise the boy in the use of the Greek alphabet.

'What is it please? I'm in charge here!'

THE
• SCHOOL DAY •

SOMETHING LIKE A SCHOOL

(An Extract from a Pupil's Diary)

[1883]

6 A.M. Got out of bed, and made a rush for old Knight's door. Old Knight is the master of our form. Shouted at him through the key-hole, and arranged a booby-trap with the coal-scuttle and a large can of water. But he sold us by letting himself down into the garden from the window, by tying his blanket, sheets, and counterpane together. However, fortunately caught sight of him when he was dangling in the air, and pelted him with tooth-brushes.

8 A.M. Breakfast. Informed Old Knight that there was a balloon and asked him to look at it. When he turned his head, we deluged him with coffee and toast-crusts.

'From what your form-master tells me, Simpson, you seem to have behaved like a big bully, with a complete disregard for life and property. Give me that peashooter.'

The Head: 'Now Wilkins, what do you know about breaking the common-room window?'

Wilkins (a K.C.'s son): 'In the first place, Sir, I deny that the window is broken. Alternatively, if it was broken, it was not by me; and, alternatively, I plead that if I did break it, it was an accident.'

Spent rest of recreation hour in making slides out of the butter-dish.

10 A.M. to 12 Noon.—At Study. Most of us reading novels the remainder playing at dumb-crambo. Fried sausages, as usual, while Old Knight was working the *pons asinorum*

Teacher: 'And Ruth walked behind the reapers, picking up the corn that they left. John, what do we call that?
John: 'Pinching.'

for us on the black-board. When we had finished our luncheons, some of us escaped by the window, and the remainder by the chimney.

2. P.M. Dinner. The usual game of pelting Old Knight with bits of potatoes, and filling his pockets with rice-pudding. Poured the beer into the Head-Master's coal-scuttle. This last feat got us into a row. We are sentenced to stay at sehool during the Christmas holidays—Old Knight is to remain with us to keep us out of mischief.

THIS HYGIENIC AGE

Swanson Junion (as the homily ends and the real business is about to start): 'Please, Sir, is it sterilised?'

18

4 P.M. TO 6.30 P.M.—More lessons and this time toffee-making. Head-Master came in and finding Billy Potter standing on his head on Old Knight's desk, kept us all in during tea-time. After this we all 'communicated our ideas' to Billy Potter, and coloured his eyes beautifully. Old Knight rather disgusted at having to mind us instead of getting his tea.

9.15 P.M. In our dormitory at last. Saw that the place was all right for the night. Screwed up all the doors belonging to the masters' rooms, piled up all the class-books on the kitchen fire, and emptied the content of the beer barrel into poor Old Knight's wardrobe. Then, having driven the cow into the best drawing room, and the sow and her little piggies into the parent's reception parlour, got into bed. As I fell off to sleep, reflected that on the whole, I had found out the way to enjoy a happy day, and wondered if Old Knight had been as fortunate.

'B-o-t, bot, t-i-n, tin, n-e-y, ney, bottiney, noun substantive, a knowledge of plants. When the boy has learned that bottiney means a knowledge of plants, he goes and knows 'em. That's our system.' *Nicholas Nickleby*

OUR BADLY USED BOYS

[1879]

The following piteous tale will but corroborate the touching accounts we have lately seen in the papers of the starving of our overworked and under-fed sons. It needs no comment:

My Dear Mama.

I am glad to see that the Guvernor has been riting to the papers about the feeding at Scools for it is disgraceful here. just fancy, we have been back a weak, and we have'n't yet seen a partridge for dinner. That old sneak Starvum is his nickname among the fellows says they are scairce.

I do'n't believe it, it is only that he is so beastly mean, then we have always had the chickens plain rosted, instead of being made eetable with

Teacher (showing picture of Adam and Eve during Scripture Lesson):
'What do we learn from this picture?'
Bright Boy: 'Eat less fruit.'

mushrooms and truffles. he actually talked of giving us goose for dinner on Michaelmas day vulgar beast. We are starved here, the potatos are always boiled, never fried in chips or Materdotel or anything tasty. They never give us peeches or apricot tart, or anything but pears and plums and grapes, it is a beastily chouse.

I felt quite ill the day after I came, I am sure it was from having so little food I could eat for I was obliged to buy a jam tart before dinner, as I had finished the hamper of Tuck I brought.

I wish the Guvernor wold write and say all scholmasters should know how to cook it would be much better than Lattin and speling and that stuff.

> *Your aff. Son*
> *O. TWIST.*

P.S.-Could you send me some of that fwa gra patty you said might tempt Aunt Lucy's appetite, it is a pitty to waist it on any-body who is not as hungery as me.

P.S.-You may send this to the times if you like.

Undergrad: 'Would you tell me, Sir, why I have been ploughed?'
Don: Sir, you have been "ploughed" (as you are pleased to
express it) for impudence.'
Undergrad: 'Oh—very sorry. I will try and be
better up in it next time!'

LAYS OF
• LEARNING •

IV. – THE FORM-MASTER.

AT Oxford University
    He worked extremely well,
He took a very high degree
    And thought himself a swell.

He came to take an Army Class
    Upon the Modern side;
They said at once he was an ass,
    And they were justified.

Proudly he marched into the room;
    The lesson was begun;
He was surprised to find by whom
    The teaching would be done.

'Buck up, Einstein!'

They taught him not to patronise,
They taught him not to nag,
That when a man is quick to rise
He's just the man to rag;

That acid irony provokes,
   Sarcastic wit annoys,
That silly elephantine jokes
   Aren't good enough for boys.

'I asked for a considered criticism of Plato,
not a diatribe'.

They taught him that it does not pay
    To cavil and suspect,
That blustering is not the way
    To make the best effect.

They taught him that it looks absurd
    To stamp about and rave
And lose one's temper; in a word.
    They taught him to behave.

And now he's winning loud applause;
    His past is growing dim;
He's making men of boys because
    They've made a man of him.

                  G.B.

'You should see the ridiculous hat my wife bought
herself yesterday.'

'Page forty, frame three – parse the
second balloon.'

LAYS OF LEARNING
XVII. – THE SCHOLAR

Emanuel Fox when at school was so good
That he won every prize that he possibly could;
He won a fine scholarship at a fine college
And continued amassing remarkable knowledge.
In each subject he took he became so immersed
That he always succeeded in getting a first;
He was learned and bright as a scholar can be
And took an amazingly brllliant degree.
And everyone said, 'Clearly Fortune ordains
That a man who has got such exceptional brains
In process of time will become very great
And play a pre-emincnt part in the State.
Before he has finished no doubt he'll have been
A Cabinet Minister, Judge or a Dean.'
But in any profession, in trade or in art,
Private means are required to tide over the start;
And Emanuel Fox, though his honours were many,
Apart from his scholarships hadn't a penny.
His authorities knew this unfortunate fact,
So they gave him advice with considerable tact.

'So you see, gentlemen, if you figure it out, the whole theory is based on an entire misconception.'

'Your soul's too artistic,' they told him, 'by far
For business or banking or even the Bar.
If you entered the House your original thought
Might lead you to say rather more than you ought;
And the same would apply should you venture to
    preach;
We think on the whole you had far better teach.'

✳ ✳ ✳ ✳ ✳ ✳

They've found him a post where the hours are so long,
The duties so dull and the pay such a song,
That he's teaching each new generation that rises
How futile it is when at school to win prizes.

G.B.

'... And finally I discovered a silly error of my own,
Mr Bartram.'

AN UNREGENERATE YOUTH

The new governess (impressively): 'O, Tommy, when *I* was a
little girl, and made a blot on my copy-book I used to cry.'
Tommy (earnestly): 'What! *really?*'
New governess (still more impressively): 'Yes–really cry!
Tommy (still more earnestly): 'What an awful little duffer you
must have been!'

THE
• GOVERNESS •

WANTED —
A GOVERNESS
[1849]

We had hoped that our occasional observations on this painful theme had shamed some and persuaded others into a more liberal course of treatment; but the following advertisement shows that the class of Governess tormentors is not yet extinct.

DAILY GOVERNESS — WANTED, in the neighbourhood of Brixton, A YOUNG LADY to take the care and education of three children from the hours of 9 till 4. She must be able to teach music and accustomed to tuition. Salary ·£12 per annum. Apply by letter, post paid, to R.H. &c.

Lady (to manager of Servants' Registry): 'I wish to obtain a new governess.'
Manager: 'Well, madam, you remember we supplied you with one only last week, but judging by the report we have received, what you really need is a lion-tamer.'

Three children for seven hours a day, at £12 per annum, will give something between a halfpenny and a penny per hour, for the tuition of each infant. The neighbourhood from which this advertisement proceeds, is quite appropriate. The governess who commits herself on those terms to Brixton is committed for hard labour,

A CONFESSION

Day Governess 'How is it that your French exercises are always done so much better than your Latin ones?"

Tommy (after considering awhile): 'I don't think Auntie knows Latin.'

indeed; and we should imagine that none but a regular 'Maid of the Mill' who had been accustomed to the tasks imposted at the House of Correction, would venture upon answering the advertisement.

CONSIDERATE – VERY

Master George (alluding to the new governess, who happened to be within hearing): 'Cross, disagreeable Old Thing, I call her!'
Miss Caroline: 'Oh, Georgy! But we ought to give way to her; she's at a very awkward age!'

Mama: 'Now go and say good-night to your governess,
like a good little girl, and give her a kiss.'
Little Puss: 'I'll say good-night, but I won't give her
a kiss.'
Mama: 'That's naughty! Why won't you give her a kiss?'
Little Puss: 'Because she slaps people's faces when they try
to kiss her.'
Mama: 'Now, don't talk nonsense; but do as
you're told.'
Little Puss: 'Well, Mummy, if you don't believe
me, —*Ask Papa!*'

'Now then, Jones Minor, what do you mean to be when you leave school?
'Please, Sir, I should like to be a doctor.'
'Well, you certainly have the qualification of illegible writing.'

BRIGHTENING SCHOOL REPORTS
[1925]

It is my intention to go down to history as the man who revolutionised report-writing in schools.'

There are roughly four styles now in vogue:

1. The Horticultural style – 'Coming on nicely' or 'Maturing well;'

2. The Puppy-training style – 'Intelligent: he responds well to correction;'

3. The Blunt style – 'He is a horrid little boy and I hate him,' after which one writes 'BUT' and makes an arrow pointing to the place where it says *The holidays begin on July 27th*;' and

4. The up-to-date Psycho-analytical style which is not much encouraged but which runs something like this:

'His listlessness is a natural protective armour against brain-fag; obviously suffering from serious neuroses; unless he goes to Madeira for a month's complete change and rest he will certainly become insane.'

5. The Illegible style.

May I tell you a little story?
There was once a headmaster who, after reading a boy's report, wrote at the bottom of it, 'Let him take heed to his pincushions.'

That, at any rate is what the boy's father made of it; so he wrote to the headmaster, who replied, 'I am indeed sorry. I wrote not "pincushions" but "pincushions."'

The word, of course, was 'penmanship'; the masters had all complained of the boy's handwriting, and the Head wrote, 'Let him take heed to his penmanship.'

This is the scheme which I propose: when the end of the term comes I am going to have the points of the mental compass printed at the top of each report; the North will represent Genius: the West, Pious Endeavour; between the two there will be a Magnetic North, which of course will represent myself: there will be correspondingly a Phlegmatic South. And so on. It will look like this:

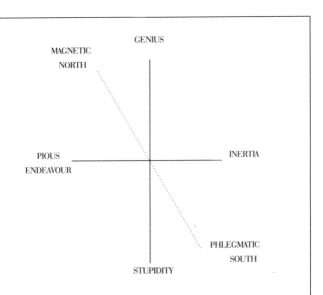

GENIUS

MAGNETIC
NORTH

PIOUS
ENDEAVOUR

INERTIA

PHLEGMATIC
SOUTH

STUPIDITY

Then all I shall have to write will be something of this sort:

Hawtrey III. Keeps a steady southwesterly course.

Jones. Last seen heading for the Phlegmatic South. Reported becalmed.

Robinson. Still endeavouring to find a N.E. Passage.

Bloggins. Believed, after a rough passage, to have discovered the South Pole.

THE NEW TYRANNY
'Of course you needn't work, Fitzmilksoppe; but *play* you
must, and *shall!*'

SCHOOL REPORTS OF THE FUTURE
[1875]

DEAR Mr. Punch,

My experience of to-day justifies me, I think, in anticipating for my Son's son, when *he* goes to a Public School, some such School Report as the enclosed.

Your obedient Servant, PETER PATERFAMILIAS

ST PAUL'S COLLEGE, EASTMINSTER.
Report for First Term of 1895.

Name – Paterfamilias Secundus.   Set II

Subject.	Place in Set.	Remarks.
I. FOOTBALL.	Back	Is not wanting in pluck – should allow more for the wind in his drop-kicks.
2. BOATING.	No.7.	Has overcome his 'screwing' propensity – hangs a little on the feather.
3. RACQUETS.		Is getting to place his balls lower, but has not yet broken himself of shutting his eyes on the stroke.

Subject.	Place in Set.	Remarks.
4. BOXING.		Striking out better from the shoulder, but still will anticipate his parry.
5. CRICKET.	Point.	A sure catch. Fair change bowler, and is improving. Might bat squarer, and wants confidence.
6. GYMNASIUM.		Parallel bars, good. will do the 'back circle' next Term.
7. ATHLETIC SPORT.	First in Mile under sixteen.	Time in long races good, but trusts too much to his spurt. Does better at long jumping than high. Putting the weight, weak.
CONDUCT.	*Coach's Report* *Housemaster's Report*	Painstaking – seems to have ambition. Obedient, except that he will practise fives in his bed-room.
HEAD-MASTER'S REMARKS ON FORM-WORK.		No observations; the weather having been so fine this Term that every day has been devoted to games.

ARNOLD BUSBY BROWN,

(Formerly Stroke of the Lady Margaret Eight, and Captain of the Cambridge Eleven)

HEADMASTER

ADVICE
TO YOUNG EXAMINEES

[Crammers and their books were denounced by the Headmaster
of Harrow at this year's [1928] meeting of the British Association.]

For any exam let us urge you to cram;
    It produces the finest effect;
Be you stupid or clever, we tell you whatever
    We think you do well to expect.

You will find, if you look on page eight of our book,
    What we feel you are certain to get:
Later on will be seen (pages ten to eighteen)
    Some questions less frequently set.

We always have reckoned on Henry the Second,
    Then study him carefully, please;
But they seem to be chary of William and Mary,
    So pay no attention to these.

You'll have nothing, we fear, on the Chartists this year,
    For they came in the paper before;
But they set in '02 – so it's long overdue –
    An account of the Hundred Years' War.

You needn't be taught why the battles were fought,
    For they never require you to say;
But remember, of course, who commanded each force
    And the year and the month and the day.

Eminent Coach (to favourite Pupil) 'Now look here Adams;
if you will only work hard with me for six months,
I promise you three years complete holiday
at Oxford!'

They have set quite a lot from the novels of Scott,
　　So it isn't a shot in the dark
To advise any boy that the name of *Rob Roy*
　　Is a means of securing a mark.

The position is worse in prescribing for verse.
　　For modern anthologies grow so;
Still we feel the young scholar maiy stakei his last
　　dollar
　　On *Maud* and *Il Penseroso*.

You will only waste time if you read them in rhyme;
　　There is much you are bound to forget:
So cut out the flummery, study our summary
　　(Price, one-and-sevenpence net).

Be always exact, for a fact is a fact,
　　And facts, you should know, are marked high.
And don't care a hoot if a lyric be beautiful –
　　Will it be set in July?

Master (to boy he has noticed looking over another's paper):
'Jones Minor, you are cribbing from Brown.'
Jones (aggrieved): 'No, Sir, I'm not. He hasn't written anything
yet that I didn't know.'

THE CRIB

He said we used a crib.
It did no good to fib.
He'd all the proof he needed:
He used the same as we did.

G.B.

'Now, Jones who defeated the Philistines?'
'I dunno, Sir. I don't follow the amateur league teams.'

QUITE CORRECT

Lady visitor (looking out at playground): 'Ah, there are all the girls, and
my little girl among them! What are they doing?'
Schoolmistress: 'They are making a snow-woman'
Lady visitor: 'A snow-what?
Schoolmistress: 'My young ladies are not allowed to make
a snow-man!'

FINISHING
• SCHOOL •

THE NEW TERM
[1927]

[The following address will not be delivered by the Headmistress
of any select finishing school in England at the beginning of the
new Term.]

My dear pupils, it gives me much pleasure to see you
once again in this Assembly Hall at the beginning of a
term which I trust will be full of interest to you and
replete with opportunities of advancement in those
branches of education so essential to the upbringing of
an English girl.

I have made it a rule, as you are aware, to ask from
each of you a letter during the summer vacation, so that
I may know how you are spending your time, with
whom you are associating and what influences are being
brought to bear upon you. Those letters I have in this

bundle in my hand, and I have few comments to make upon them. Let me remind Phyllis Mayne, however, that 'accommodation' is spelt with two 'm's,' and when Barbara Dallys describes one of her new frocks a 'p-u-rfectly fa-s-cinating' she is taking an unwarrantable liberty with written English. I am sorry, but Barbara must write out 'perfectly fascinating' fifty times.

Swedish Exercise Instructress: 'Now, Ladies, if you only follow my directions carefully, it is quite possible that you may become even as I am!'

Yvonne Ducane tells me she has been to Knokke, in Belgium, for a month. I must protest. I shall next hear that one of you has been to Margate or Blackpool. Gladys Soames chose Deauville more wisely. She need not however have told me that evening-frocks are being worn an inch and a half longer there. I am aware of that. I am not altogether sure that I approve of her going to the Casino, but as she *did* go I am glad she won one hundred and eighty francs at roulette. She consistently backed the *première douzaine*. Unexciting but sound.

Enid Garratt has kept up her tennis form and won the Junior Open Singles at Palton-on-Sea. Good, Enid. You tell me the prize was a powder-puff in the form of a Russian Dancer. Let me see it and I will tell you if it is suitable for your dressing-table.

Congratulations, Christine Graham, on your brother's engagement, especially as his fiancée is one of the Hailmans of Hopton Court. You will find them in Burke's Landed Gentry. I am sorry they were 'sloppy' and that the billiard room was practically out-of-bounds for you every evening. But 'sloppy' is a word you simply must not use. So much for the moment for the letters.

Now as to the new term. There is but little change in the curriculum, but we welcome a new addition to the staff, Miss Messenger, who will teach Calligraphy and the latest developments of the Flat Charleston. Miss Robartes will continue to take French Conversation and the Informatory Double at Auction Bridge, which some of you have not thoroughly grasped yet; while Miss Gross will specialise this term in the covered tennis-court on the 'Backhand Volley' and the 'Position of the Feet in the Overhead Service.' I shall of of course take the Deportment Classes as usual.

One or two new rules I have had to make, which you will see posted up. I summarise the principal:–

1. Fashion papers are not to be bought. The necessary and best are in the school reading-room.

2. Lip-sticks and smoking, with or without cigarette-holders, are absolutely forbidden.

3. Face-powder will be provided and no other kinds are to be purchased. They are frequently adulterated and chemically impure.

I am glad to welcome the new pupils, especially Marie Palien, niece of the Comte de Gissoure; Natalie Vane, daughter of the Rear-Admiral of that name, and Suzanne Cloute, whose father was very justifiably made a baronet recently. May they and all of you work hard and reap the advantages which it is the constant aim of myself and my staff to provide! Good-night.

UNIFORMLY CHIC

The standardization of schoolgirls' uniform has been provoking indignant comment from many women journalists. They feel that girls should wear what they like in the few years left to them before they come under M. Dior's iron rule.

21 October 1953

'So far as I can see, Mr Potson,
you haven't altered a scrap.'

THE OLD
· SCHOOL ·

A FRANK ADDRESS TO
THE OLD SCHOOL
[1953]

My dear boys, it was kind and wise of your Head-master to choose me to address you. Just when I was reaching the port stage of my excellent dinner with him last night, you were supposed to be dropping off to sleep in your dormitories and those of you who had not strings fastened to your toes to wake you if you snored, or who were not suspended by your feet from the rafters for not being good enough at football, were no doubt trying to get some rest.

I like an early cup of tea in the morning, and at seven, when mine was brought, the well-known sound of the bell woke you from dreams of home to the more familiar white-washed walls of school, the rows of iron bedsteads, each bed with its pale burden under the red blankets. I think there must be some educational supply company which has a monopoly of school bells. Their note is always the same, not so irritating as the telephone, but more terrifying; not so mellow as the church bell but more ominous; not so evocative of excitement as a fire alarm, but conveying the relentless monotony to which it calls you.

As I lay in bed wondering what I was going to say to you, I heard your merry little feet pattering over cool linoleum to some healthy cold tubs to freshen you up for another day's work. It was raining hard outside and I was imagining that you would soon have to be hurrying away from a hasty breakfast, across wet courts and under windy arches to classrooms smelling of ink, old boots, old biscuits and bat oil, there to bluff your way through the morning, trying to prevent your form master finding out that you had not done last night's preparation. By this time my breakfast was brought to me in bed on a tray, grapefruit, eggs and bacon; toast, coffee, marmalade, and *no porridge whatsoever.*

Do not imagine, however, I am trying to make you envious. I have got up after a nice hot bath and at a rea-

Master (after the event): 'Do you know young man, that this pains me much more than it does you?'
The Terror: 'No, I didn't know, Sir. But if that assertion genuinely expresses your considered opinion I feel very much better.'

sonable hour and can see things clearly. You will only be able to have these privileges by becoming so ill that you have to be moved to the sanatorium. But even then you will get well again and it will be doubly hard to adjust yourselves to the rigours of the school curriculum.

And, dear boys, let me remind you of the date. We are early in October. Christmas is a long way off. The

'Gosh! Are you P.K.'s mater?'

Christmas holidays are short; then comes that terrible term when it is so cold that you have chilblains on your toes as well as on your fingers. Then there are even shorter holidays at Easter and after that the long, long summer term with its unspeakably boring hours of grilling cricket followed by the dangers and the duckings of the bathing place.

But I am anticipating. I wonder how many of you will survive unscathed until the summer term? Looking round at this sea of faces, I wonder how many of you will be expelled; how many times each of you will be beaten by the prefects for leaving your clothes about, by your housemasters for not doing enough work, by the Headmaster for more serious crimes. Some of you I see already have spots. During the term, owing to the difference in the food from what you are accustomed to at home, these spots will grow angrier and boils will appear on the backs of your necks. But these are not complaints bad enough to earn you a rest in the sanatorium.

Well, it is time for me to go now. Your Headmaster has kindly put his car at my disposal to take me to the airport. I am taking a 'plane to a diplomatic mission in Bermuda. Besides having ample private means, I am paid by the Minister of Commonwealth Relations, for whom I am a sort of roving ambassador, at £5,000 a year with hotel bills and expenses extra. I shall stay at the best place in whatever is the capital of Bermuda, and I shall be away for some months as my work is of national, nay global, significance. Perhaps your Headmaster would like me to talk to you again next summer and if I have the time I will come. But I am a busy man.

JOHN BETJEMAN

'I trust, Mickleton Minimus, that you will not have the impertinence to contradict me when I say that I perceive an element of defiance in your present bearing.'